We Are Not the Same ☾

Presentation by *BookLeaf Publishing*

Web: www.bookleafpub.com

E-mail: info@bookleafpub.com

ISBN: 9789363316058

First edition 2024

ACKNOWLEDGEMENT

I spent 8 years of my life feeling lost, and this series has brought me back to myself. I lost myself the day my mother passed away, and this collection has helped me reclaim my power. Her passion for literature and the arts instilled in me a deep appreciation for the power of words to heal, to express, and to connect. I have rediscovered myself because she taught me it was possible.

PREFACE

As I reflect on the journey that led to the creation of this collection, "We Are Not the Same," I am reminded of the profound power of poetry as a means of expression, healing, and transformation. This collection of poetry was born from the depths of personal upheaval and the journey toward reclaiming identity.

"We Are Not The Same" became a sanctuary—a space where I could feel what I felt without being told I was wrong or less than. In my journey, vulnerability is transformed into strength, and rawness finds solace in the beauty of language. This is an invitation to walk alongside me and to witness the unfolding of a narrative that speaks to the universal human quest for understanding, acceptance, and ultimately, redemption.

Shameless

I'm not really sure what's happening with people
and the amount of shame they feel for being who
they are.

I can't live in that world, and I certainly won't go
back 25 years to empathize.
The best line I ever heard was, "I follow my
whims unapologetically," and I very much do.

I am comfortable with who I am, even all the
messy parts, and I make no apologies.
I live as purely and as raw as I can, despite the
shame around me.
Your shame cannot be mine because I carry
enough of my own, but we are not the same.

My shame comes from lies—a person I cannot
be for you because I no longer live in a closet.
I pretended for years—for you—and I feel
shame.
It is not my shame because we are not the same.

My shame comes from not being able to
speak—I allowed you to destroy my name.
Was I the pursuer?

That seems like a joke as we stood by my car
and you told me you had feelings for me.
But I didn't know the extent of your shame, and
had I known, I would have walked away,
because I only have one name.

I tell myself a million stories—
I excuse you and I excuse her, but there are no
real excuses.
We are not the same!

With her, I shared years… I cannot get them
back.
With you, I shared my soul—an honesty that
forced me to step outside my walls. I will not
apologize, and I will not be ashamed.

I stepped outside only to face the reality that you
lied—to me or to him or to yourself.
Instead of accepting what you felt—intense and
raw—you made it about me.
We are not the same.

While I have seen the violence of battlefields,
the hate in the eyes of women who claimed to
love me, the darkness of a hole that seemed to
suck me in and was never going to release me, I
have also experienced joys that cannot be
properly put into words…

But I will try: the loving arms of a woman who
would give her life for me; the failure of a man
who tried to find redemption when I needed
him; the birth of sons who bear my name—their
glorious arrivals in the world opened up a piece
of me that brings me to tears at night as I watch
them sleep, knowing the world is theirs for the
taking; the unconditional love of friends who
would walk through hell and back with me; a job
that fills my soul… because I realize that I get to
live on in them.

I am truly blessed because I reflect on how far
I've come.
I have been bruised and beaten, but I remain
intact—we are not the same.

I've Learned

I've learned that no matter how much I endure, I
can stand tall.
I've learned that if I give up, the world keeps
going.
This year has taught me to smile and take in the
simple moments—
To laugh, to talk, to take a minute to be at peace.

I've learned that everyone has a story—some
good and some bad—
I've learned that on my bad days, I can still be
my best.
And that on my best days, I'm a force to be
reckoned with.

I've learned to keep going despite rough waters
and to know that even the bad times have to end.
I've learned to accept happiness even when my
world is dark—
That I have the power to make things better.

I've learned that time heals all wounds and that
even though the scars remain, they fade.
I've learned to live on my own because in the
end, you always wake up with yourself.

So, of all the lessons I've learned in life, I've
learned to love myself.

5

You

You appeared and changed my being—
It was subtle and quick and I didn't realize.
My eyes are open and I am seeing—
All the things I'm forced to recognize.

My choices or lack there of—I try to analyze.
Can things be so easy?
It feels surreal.
I deeply smile—no real surprise.
Unafraid and free—I embrace what I feel.

Aware that I am flawed—I attempt to heal.
I learn to adjust—your kindness and strength
feed my soul.
I open up and face my truth—I learn to deal.
I've trusted, invested, been outright
detested—the pain takes its toll.

A believer in all that transcends—
Hoping and praying—all that doesn't break
bends.

Her

I am the pieces of her she left behind.
The pieces I wish I could forget because the
bruises are still visible.

I remember the look in her eyes, but how I long
to forget.
The sound of her voice terrified me, and
sometimes I romanticize her—
She was so many wonderful things… but not to
me!

She was Sunday… a time for peace and
rejuvenation, but instead I always felt anxious.
She was a drink or two that turned into anger,
and I questioned if I was even sane as I spent the
night apologizing.
She was fear and anxiety—but she was wrapped
in tattoos and curves.
My body pressed against hers—
Possibly peace?
But not even that was truth.

I lived in a state of fear, but that's all I've ever
known—this fear that she would leave or maybe
it was a fear that she wouldn't and I couldn't.

Sometimes I convinced myself that I was in
love, but love does not induce fear—
I realize now that she was trauma.
And now I spend my time in therapy discussing
her—as always, I forget me.

Time

Maybe time has made it impossible to
remember,
But how could I forget?
When you see what I've seen—
How could I be different?

Harsh words, the sound of hands… I'm huddled
in a corner.
The perception of a child—distorted and
confused about love.

A strength I later come to recognize with a
goodbye.
An anger I hope I never have… I am different.

A smallness that I understand with actions I
could never justify.
My small crippled my ability to love.

He was wild and unaware—
And all I could do was stare as the milk covered
the floor.

Truth is what we never spoke of.
He was gone, you were fierce, and I was afraid.

The Walk

I remember the day as clearly as yesterday.
We walked a distance from each other, stopping
in front of a gray van.
You spoke fearlessly, and in that moment, I
wanted to be you.

I think of you all the time.
Those words screamed of unhealthiness—
I loved hearing them,
Toxic, fulfilling, everything I needed.

You spoke of care, feeling, not wanting to be
afraid, and I believed.
Our talks on the phone, the look in your eyes as
I walked into the room, that weird day you
walked in while I wondered what you wanted.
You didn't speak that day;
I just continued as usual.
I wish I had spoken.

We
Were
Strange.

A strangeness I longed to understand.
A peace that would happen in your presence…
But something changed…
Was it you?
Was it my perception of you?

You gave me space—enough to have me
appreciate your absence and my lack of
confusion.
You gave me space—I missed our toxicity.

But then I discovered what you'd been doing.
I didn't have words;
I made a joke—there's always a joke to be
made.
I was hurt.
You tried to reassure me of your intentions, but
at that point, I was broken.

You broke me.

We were strange, and I hated that walk.

Jealous

I was already feeling your loss…
I needed to feel something other than this, so I
did what I do best.
I looked for something—and I found it.

There you were, active within 2 hours, and it hit
me that you were dating.
The thought of that made me sick!
Someone else would hold you after bliss, and
then it hit me that you never let me hold you.
For three years, I longed to hold you in my arms,
and while I did—
You never were mine; I just borrowed you from
your husband.

I questioned my whole being at that moment.
I couldn't help but click on your profile, filled
with pics from things we did together—
The parade we went to with my sons,
The Renaissance Faire we strolled around all
day,
The fancy dinner we went to after my divorce,
The pics you sent me while sunbathing—all lies.
You never were mine; I just borrowed you from
your husband.

I am always the problem.
And maybe I was because you said you were
mine, and I wanted to believe you were mine,
but you didn't come home to me at night.
I was the person you called before you made it
home to tell me you loved me…
I had a distorted definition of love.
You never were mine; I just borrowed you from
your husband.

I remember nights dancing and nights spent in
my apartment that ended with your back to me,
and whenever I tried to hold you, you'd push me
away.
Maybe I needed too much—
It feels like I often needed too much—
But you said you were mine.
You never were mine; I just borrowed you from
your husband.

I waited and waited…
Three years I can't get back—
My ego, my pride abandoned long ago as I sat
there waiting for you to file for divorce—
Waiting and waiting for you to come—
Waiting and waiting for our time to be together.
It never came because when I told her about us,
you grew angry.

You never were mine; I just borrowed you from
your husband.

I was there while you lived a life that didn't
involve me.
You don't feel my loss because I was never your
day-to-day.
You don't feel my loss because you're not
forced to look at my bathrobe or house
slippers… that's my cross to bear.
I remove the pieces of you that exist in my space
for the millionth time because this pattern was a
familiar one.
But this time feels final—
I'm reminded…
You never were mine; I just borrowed you from
your husband.

Poison

We sit around and talk for hours—
There's an easiness in one aspect of our
relationship.
A gentleness that is hard to find in this chaotic
world.
You bring me peace in so many ways, but all the
signs are there.

Your emotional level is at zero.
Your walls are so high sometimes, and I'm too
old to climb a ladder.
You lure me in and push me away…
It's exhausting.
I enjoy the ride because I can fantasize about
what we could be, but the truth is—Hard.
Nothing.

I currently live in truth because you haven't
painted a web of illusion around me in quite
some time.
I long for illusion because in that world, we are
together.
In reality, I am alone.
But I am alone in both.

Why is being alone so hard for me?
I sit with this big question—
I hate big questions.
I find the answers buried deep inside, but
rewiring my brain takes time.
I work on connecting to myself and feeling
connected to the universe.

But I can't help but come back for a drink from
your cup—
Maybe I love the taste of poison.

Mi Mejor Venganza

My greatest revenge is not dating the hot,
younger, thinner version of you without
attachments,
But rather loving myself enough to not want you
or anyone like you.
I believe you don't realize how absolutely toxic
you were—
You'll say it was me.

I needed too much.
I had expectations.
I wanted to be close.
I expected to be a part of your life.
Maybe I sabotaged us.
Maybe by wanting real commitment, I ruined us.
That was never your real purpose.

I couldn't see it for what it was—
I didn't realize I was the fool waiting around.
Hindsight is 20/20—
And I feel bad for the next person you're with—
They will feel so amazing hearing your words.
Talk of loyalty as you keep them on the outside
of your life.

But you'll give them a small window to peer
through so they can have some hope.

I stood outside that window on a bench that I
had to drag over, stood on my tippy toes with a
rope around my neck 8 feet above the ground.
A window that will never open for them because
in actuality you have nothing to offer.
You speak of truth when all you do is weave a
web of lies—so calculated that you might
believe your words have value.

Your words and actions are hurtful…
You were hurtful as you immersed yourself in
my life and watched as I hung with a rope
around my neck, desperately trying to keep my
balance until I just couldn't anymore.

You stepped outside only to kick the bench out
from under me.
You were always good at kicking me when I was
down.
Where exactly were you when I needed you?
Home, with your husband.

You speak of truth and loyalty—
That's just it—all you do is SPEAK.

Unreliable Narrator

I need to speak my truth because once I say it, it
has been said and then I can't go back.
Maybe I am not ready, or in some way, maybe
I've never been more ready.
I need to not go back…
Because I'm changed and I can't pretend I'm not.

I believe the universe holds power—
I release this into the universe and let it be…

I like knowing that you know what the voice in
my head sounds like.
I like knowing that after a long weekend or after
a really bad night,
I will hear the sound of your laughter or the very
distinct sound of your voice.
I like knowing that we exist in the same space
because for some reason you calm my soul.
I like that you take direction well and recognize
that hugs should last a minimum of 10 seconds,
which might make you the second-best hugger I
know.

I created space because of her—
I regretted my decision.

But we must live with our choices.
I don't like the space you created when I didn't
want space but you chose to push away.
I don't like the idea of months without you.
I don't like that I won't hear from you because
your ego is bigger than mine.
I don't like that I even care because I've worked
so hard to condition myself to not care.

I sit with why…
I sit with my anxiety…
With the pounding of my heart…
With this feeling in my gut that almost cripples
me…
I sit with truth and I deny it because I can't not
know what I know in my heart, and I spend each
day trying to be typical.

I can't deny that the feel of your arms around my
neck felt as natural as the air that fills my lungs
or the feel of the sun on my skin.
I can't deny that as I wrapped my arms around
your waist, I wanted to cry.
And then I looked at you and you were crying…
I don't know why but I wonder.

I can no longer wonder or read the situation the
way that suits my narrative.

My narrative is filled with inconsistencies
because of you—
I'm an unreliable narrator!

While this adds layers of complexity and
intrigue to a narrative, one cannot truly discern
the truth.
So I speculate, but our narratives don't match
up—
How can they when it is actually you who is
unreliable?

The Kindness of Friends

I'm reminded of who I was,
The me who existed before you and before the
several versions of you that I dated.
I can pinpoint the relationship that caused the
end of who I was, and progressively, the
relationships got worse.

I once thought I deserved this—
I had to be better so you all could be better.
I learned to shut my mouth.
I wanted to speak, and I chose not to because
that came with consequences.
The bruises I was ashamed to speak of, or a
silence that broke my soul.

"Don't even fucking exist in my presence."
It was a cycle—so abusive that I believed it was
love.
When I spoke of it, the looks on people's faces
were disturbing.
I realized other people don't live like this.
I can't even admit it fully yet because I don't
play the victim well, despite your claims, and
the level of shame is immense.

I am strong, confident, and assertive.
But in this cycle, I am 5 years old, huddled in a
corner, waiting in fear for the fireworks that
would leave me out of breath and suffocating.

I can no longer live in fear, so I remember who I
was before the cycle started.
I learn to be alone again because I have always
been good company.
I sit around with people I love and who love me,
despite the several times I've distanced myself
in this cycle, and pray that I can go back to who
I was.
Maybe I can't go back—years of damage make
it hard to undo—so I become a different version
of myself.
The version that recognizes that while I miss
you, it is not you I miss but the familiar.
Your chaos is familiar, and I passively stayed
until I found my voice and left long before it
ended.

Sleeping in my car changed me that night.
Your harsh reaction to my opposition—I didn't
like what you did.
Your eyes filled with hate.
I tried to defuse it —
I often tried to defuse it, but my weakness fueled
your rage.

I was scared—
Too proud to admit that I was.
190 pounds of terrified, a stark contrast to the
60-pound version of myself, but I see the
similarities.

So now, I surround myself with joy.
I am fully present in the moment.
The anxiety of how you'll respond has ceased.
I do the things that bring me peace while I miss
the chaos.
I realize that I'm damaged, but I will heal
myself—
The kindness of friends will see me through.

8 Years Later

I never allowed myself to properly feel her loss.
I immediately kept myself busy—there's so
much to do and so much to plan for.
I needed to prepare for the funeral; it was Easter.
I had to prepare to return to work; it was
summer and the house had to be cleaned.
I had to sell the house in Belleville.
I was going to Spain, I was going to Thailand.
Construction had to start on Coles.
I had to plan a wedding,
I had to plan the birth of my son—
So busy, so busy.
The hallways at Coles Street needed to be
redone, the second floor needed to be renovated.
I had to prepare to sell the house, I was buying a
new one and that took time to prepare.
I had to prepare for my second son.
Then Covid made it impossible to keep busy, but
I still did.

Even now I write about all the things I did to
avoid an attempt to not feel.
I never let myself feel the loss—
But after everything has settled and I'm away
for a spiritual retreat to restore my soul,

I cried for her.
There was nothing to distract me, even though I
looked.

We sat and spoke of our mothers and sadly, I
could not keep the tears from forming, which
happens every single time I mention her.
Maybe it's easier not to mention her, but in order
to heal and grow, I have to accept—

That I will never hear her voice again.
That we will never have a talk.
That she will never call me to say hello.
That she is gone and I never made her proud.
That she will never get to look at my sons.
That I left a lot to be desired.
That I couldn't stop her from dying.
That is the reality—she died and I sat there and
could do nothing.

I try so hard to keep things in order, to maintain
a semblance of control.
But in that moment on a Friday morning, when I
got the call that she was put in a coma, I was
defenseless.
I was defenseless when I arrived at that hospital
to discuss options.
I was defenseless when I was forced to make
decisions that I knew meant it was over.

i was small—
I again had to sit by and do nothing because I
was defenseless.
I watched her help herself during my youth—she
was not defenseless.
She was everything I wanted to be and in that
moment as I made decisions.
I had to tell my brother on the happiest day of
his life because his daughter was born that our
mother was going to die—I was defenseless
again.

It was all the noise around me that I could
control, and I did.
I distracted myself only to get that call on a
Thursday morning from my Aunt Betty that she
was gone.
In that moment, I hated Betty.
I hated her for waking me up as a child to tell
me Raphael was gone, and I hated that I knew
what it meant when the phone rang that early
and it was Betty.

I didn't cry that morning because I had nothing
left.
I had woken up so many times while sleeping,
suffocating and in tears, that I couldn't cry.

Things needed to be handled, and I dressed to
get my brother and make our way to see her one
last time in that hospital in NY.

It was the longest ride of my life, and I walked
into her room.
She had a white sheet covering her face.
The air felt thick, and I removed the sheet while
my brother and I cried and said our goodbyes.
That was the last time we would all sit on the
bed together.
That was the last time we would all be alone
together.

I didn't need to speak—because she knew.
And I can say that while I feel like I
disappointed her and she wasn't proud, I know
that's not true.
I disappointed myself because I couldn't save
her, and this time, she couldn't save herself.
I have seen that woman walk through
fire—literal fire—as a child, when she entered a
burning building to get the elderly neighbor
upstairs, Mary.
How can someone who walks through fire just
die?

I have been unwilling to accept, and now I must
because I am stuck.

I am plagued by shame and guilt, and that shame
and guilt cripple my ability to love.
I cannot have someone I love so much leave me
again.

I hold my sons—I remind them of her so often
so that they know her—
The woman who walked through fire and who
loved us so fiercely.
I am reminded that she lives in me, and as I hold
my sons—I know they know that they come
from greatness.
I know they can feel the greatness as we share
family hugs and take family walks, and have
random chip parties while cuddled in bed.
They come from greatness because while I have
not walked through fire, I have walked through
hell and back and I'm still standing.

And as life throws things my way, I'm reminded
that nothing can be as bad as the day I had to
bury my mother.
The only thing worse than burying my mother is
knowing that I couldn't save her.
It was not my job to save her—It was in God's
hands.
I am not God, but I pray for peace, and 8 years
later, I found that peace on top of a mountain.

I stood up there and watched God, and I knew
my mom was watching me.
I couldn't save her, but once again, she saved
me.

My Happy Place

I always found peace here—It was my place,
and while I've shared this spot with others, it
remains mine.
The water crashing on the rocks as I stare at
Lady Liberty reminds me that freedom comes
with a price.
I am humbled by that notion, and I never take
my freedom for granted.
My body glistening in sweat, I'm thankful for the
feel of the sun on my face and the slight breeze
that caresses my body as I start to heat up.

I am in this moment.
I am the sun that shines brightly.
I stare at the sun only to close my eyes and still
see it—
I watch it fade away, and I sit in darkness for a
minute, hearing the sounds all around me.
The waves on the rocks, the helicopters
overhead, the birds chirping, the voices of
people intruding on my solitude.
I am the sounds I hear—
As I open my eyes and take in the visualization
of the sounds that surround me.

I am the breeze that can come and go as it
pleases.

I am free—of you, of her, of these scorpions that
plagued me throughout the day.
In this solitude, I'm reminded that you never
came with peace and she brought me momentary
peace; it too was short-lived.
It was chaos; oh, how I loved it.
It is not what I need—
This is what I need.
I need to know my place in the world—
And all I know now is freedom.
Freedom comes with a price—
A price I'd gladly pay with my life to never lose
it again.

The Stage Magician

I can't help but be curious about you.
There's that part of me that just wants so badly
to be a part of your day.
I realize I'm not and that I never was.
I see that you're living your life—a life that
doesn't involve me, and a piece of me is sad.
Your life never involved me, even though
occasionally you would fill me in.

I never got to sit around and laugh with your
friends.
I never got to experience the day-to-day with
you, and I'm hurt.
But what did I miss?
I missed your negative attitude.
You always found a way to bring down the
mood—
A problem, there was always a problem.
My world doesn't function like that.
I find solutions, and you enjoy living in
problems.

I find myself thinking about how you're living
your best life, and I want that for you, but I
know it's not real.

Your pictures and posts give the illusion.
You always were quite the magician—but I
know the truth.
That bunny that lives up your sleeve is dead, but
you manage to disguise his death for others, and
they believe your illusion.
I want truth, and you are all smoke and
mirrors—conjuring up stories that seem
convincing to the naked eye.
I have always been much deeper—
I see beyond the scope of others, so I see you
raw and bruised—you could never get me to
believe.

Maybe now, with my absence, you have found
that happiness.
Maybe me seeing you was something that you
didn't need or want.
Maybe the intensity shattered your illusion, and
you needed me to disappear.
But you have to know that while you've
managed to put me in a box—I won't be there
again when you try to get me to appear.
I have managed to somehow get myself out of
the coffin with the nails you put in it.

I am gone.

The Tree

It stands as majestic and peaceful as ever, with its branches like arms stretched out to the heavens.
I see myself in its glory—having weathered many storms.
While it appears slightly battered, it manages to thrive despite the changing seasons and the impact that shows.

If I surround myself with chaos, I am chaos.
I am learning to forgive myself.
Now that the noise has faded and I'm forced to sit with absence, I've realized I'm more than okay.
The storms have passed, and I, of course, always knew how to bend and sway; it was the perfect storm.
While I enjoyed the chaos, it was temporary, and the calm and sun would come again.
I was not the chaos—you were.

And while I was a willing participant, I shouldn't have been.
I'm learning to forgive myself.

I release any hurt I feel because I was naive
enough to believe—
This was really about ego.
I wanted to be the person you chose because I
needed to feel like I mattered.
While you did choose me, it came with
compromises I couldn't make because it is not
who I was born to be.
I cannot compromise with my expectations or
my boundaries because I would have to feel like
I'm less than to make this work.

I wanted what you offered to be enough, but it
wasn't, and I clung to the hope that things would
change.
I clung to the hope that it could be different, but
I knew all along that a leaf could never be a
branch, and a branch, while it might be strong
enough to hold me when I needed, could never
be a root.
I'm learning to forgive myself.

I watched the leaf fly off the tree, and every
piece of me wanted to run after it, climb back up
the rungs, and place it back where it belonged.
But it didn't belong there, and I'm learning to
forgive myself.

So I watched it blow away with the wind, and I
smiled.
The tree stands tall, there for years to come
without it—and while it has changed—it is still
as beautiful as ever.
I am learning to forgive myself because I can't
hold on to leaves.
The wind forces me to bend and sway, and new
adventures await me while I work on
forgiveness.

The Stages

I forgot I had a choice.
Relationships can be funny in that regard.
I had to keep the peace.
I had to make sure you stayed, but at what cost?

I forgot I had a choice.
I let you push my boundaries further and further.
Eventually, I couldn't even see them in the
distance.
Did I deserve this?
I couldn't even look at myself because the
bruises that covered my chest brought shame.
You mocked me about being the victim, but I
was, and you made me feel like the aggressor on
more nights than I care to remember.

Did I deserve this…because I was inconsistent,
because I spoke to others, because I had support,
because I was tired, because I didn't invest too
much even though I had laid my soul at your
feet, because I loved you more than I loved
myself?

But I never did play the victim well.

While you weren't the first to violate my soul,
others before you had also done the same.
You were the first to claim you loved me
immensely every morning and promise that
you'd be different.

You now joined a line of monsters that lived in a
closet I had shut away because of shame.
Was I really that unlovable?
I sat with that—maybe I deserved the violence
because I couldn't be what you needed me to
be—that distorted thinking needed to be healed.
I was never the violence; it was a part of my
surroundings, and I allowed it to become my
reality because the monster lived in you, and it
terrified me.

I was my own monster—
I needed something to save me from myself
because I would allow this to continue.
It was a pattern—with you and her, and honestly,
I can't even see the difference between the two
of you.
In the end, you looked like her, and now when I
see her, I see her demons and self-hate, and I
steer clear of that rage.
I will not be friends with the monster that once
lived in my closet.

I will not make excuses for your rage, your hate,
your inadequacies…
I will finally speak my truth—it was abuse.

I lived in fear because I saw myself unworthy of
something real, but now I live in truth.
I speak to women, and I learn to appreciate an
honest conversation.
But I still live in fear because no one tells you
they are going to hit you.
I still live in fear because no one tells you that
they are going to manipulate you.
I still live in fear because no one tells you they
are going to emotionally abuse you with distance
and ignore your messages until it suits them.
Maybe the truth is that I just attract abuse.

For now, I am fine walking alone—because I
cannot and will not take another round of this
cycle.
I grow and learn to trust again.
I remember my worth—that air of confidence
returns without you.
I don't ever have to be afraid because I will
never betray myself again.

Careless People

The temperature reads 93°F in the shade.
For a moment, I wait for someone to pass by to
help me,
But I'm crippled—my body covered in sweat—I
want to just sleep.
I can't breathe.
I can feel myself struggle.
I'm dizzy.
I just want some water and some air.
I think I may have passed out but I can't be
certain because at this point nothing seems real.

You finally enter the car and with the door ajar,
you put it on—
The burst of air flows through the vents and for
a brief second I am saved.
As quickly as I feel relief,
I'm back into distress because the car is off
again and you've shut the door.
I glance around for the keys—nothing.
My hand reaches up to the handle because I
seem to have enough strength to be lured back
because you knocked on the driver's side
window and held a finger in the air signaling
that you'd just be one more second.

And so, I wait while I feel myself slipping away.
I wait as I can feel myself dying or am I already
dead?

My head starts to hurt—
I'm completely drenched in sweat again and my
dizziness has returned but here you come again
but this time you enter the car and the warm air
hits me—it feels like heaven.
Funny what desperation allows us to believe.
I was just in a different degree of hell but the
exhaustion caused confusion.
I realized that no one was going to pass by.
I had to do this alone—story of my life.
I was often alone even while in a crowded room.
This time the door was ajar because in your
haste to leave, you carelessly swung the door.
You always were careless, you and your husband
must have sat at the table that night eating cold
chicken and drinking ale.
I was the mistress laying on the road except I
was able to get up.
I walked away covered in sweat and gasping for
breath but I managed to walk away.
And while my mind travels back and forth
between heaven and hell—
I'm reminded that you both were unable to clean
up the mess, which is why you're still in the
house together.

I managed to clean up the mess and now I can
even speak of it without fear.

43

49

She asked me what I needed from her.
I don't think I've ever had a woman ask me
that—she was genuine.
I told her that I needed kindness.
She made a smart remark about being able to
offer me basic human kindness—she was a little
sassy.
It was sexy, but that seemed familiar.

We spoke, and it was raw and genuine—I
appreciated her kindness.
I appreciated her ability to ask questions.
I appreciated the way she spoke of my
arrogance—turns out that one might be true.
I appreciated her willingness to meet my hand at
the check when it arrived.
I appreciated the walk we took and pretending to
watch the soccer match at the bar.
I appreciated sitting on her balcony overlooking
the park and her putting her hair up and
throwing on a t-shirt.
I appreciated how she felt when we hugged
goodnight and how she was shorter than me.
I appreciated how she held onto me just a little
longer because she knew I needed that.

Of all the things I appreciated that night, I
appreciated that we went our separate ways.
She remained in her apartment, and I returned to
mine—to look forward to another day of
kindness.

Random

You disappeared.
It's been weeks, and you enter as if we are
picking up a conversation from the night before.
I continue with my day—the kindness of friends
and playdates takes over.
I mention you sent me a message—laughter fills
the air—it does seem like a joke.
I answer questions about the other one, but I
have no real answers other than she's still using
my EZPass—maybe ask your husband to pay
that bill because I canceled that tag effective
immediately.
But I'm not laughing because neither one of you
amuses me.

I've moved to a new phase in my life—kindness.
I realize that you're damaged; I can forgive.
I realize that she's angry; I can forgive.
But in all the forgiveness I offer, I do not offer
redemption.
You cannot return—we are not the same.
I would have responded in the past—allowed the
foolishness to continue for at least two rounds of
texting, but I am not the same.

I am bothered—I recognize that, but I forgive
myself for being bothered.
I haven't spoken your name in weeks, and I
survived.
This breadcrumb today will remain on the field
for the birds—not for me.
I am not looking to be stonewalled or
breadcrumb-ed or whatever other term is used to
describe what avoidants tend to do.
I now know my worth—I've come a long way!

I still remember the only line you shared from
the poem you claimed you started to write for
me.
I wanted that poem.
I needed that poem.
So now I've written myself twenty-one.
That poem was never coming—not from you
and not from her.
The poem was always inside of me.

I am the rhythm in each line—the enjambment
that carries on until its end-stopped, and I've left
the reader questioning—self, life, and ideals.
I am the caesura that was placed with purpose so
the reader could properly feel the emotion, and I
could take a second to catch my breath from
trauma.

My verses paint a picture of my process—the
hurt and devastation coupled with progress and
growth.
That text kicked up a lot of feelings today, but
I'm working on forgiving myself.
You are who you are—she is who she is—I am
who I am—the three of us are not the same.
We are not the same.
Here's my arrogance shining through—I was
always better!

Fire

I set the house on fire.
I watched it burn as I sat in the yard.
I was always drawn to fire.
It had power, which I always longed for.
I wanted to have some control, so on a May afternoon in 2021, I poured gasoline around the exterior.
In June of 2021, I walked inside covered in gasoline and stood by an open flame.
I didn't blow up, and while I was suffocating from the fumes, I survived.

I continued to tempt fate, walking around exposed and completely drenched, but I managed to survive.
For years, I walked around waiting for the flames to consume me, but they never did.
I forgot I was covered in gasoline.
I walked right into the open flame and managed to walk out, unharmed.
I was slightly scorched, which surprised me a little, but that was probably because I believed she was different.
As always, I was wrong.

I made a decision to set the house on fire, and on
a June afternoon in 2024, I lit a match and sat in
the yard.
I watched the house burn, and I smiled.
I love to rebuild.

The Process

The Beginning—

I needed to distract myself.
While searching Instagram, I saw a challenge.
I decided to explore it, and it gave me a chance
to delve into the emotions that were flowing.
I often encourage writing as a form of
expression but don't always practice what I
preach.
I needed to release, so I started writing, and
when I did, my life changed instantly.
This release meant that I could express my
emotions without constant contradiction.
My ideas were not distorted—they were an
interpretation of the reality I experienced.
I needed to remind myself that my emotions
were valid, and your words were those of a
woman filled with anger.
I could never understand that anger because it
doesn't exist in me.
You had lost control.
I had to reclaim my sense of self—and after
years of the same chaotic routine, it had to end.

The Middle—

I'm halfway through my journey, and I've
learned a lot about myself.
I've learned a lot about my
relationships—present, past, and my
expectations for the future.
I know the cycle, and I need it to be different
because my soul can't survive another round.
I embrace the love that has always been there
because I lead a charmed life and release all the
anger and darkness that comes from those who
claim to love me but secretly—or maybe not so
secretly—hate me.
That coldness and harshness are not for me. I am
warm and light.
While I might not always know my path, I am
aware that all paths lead to something bigger.
This type of "love" is not love but rather a
self-fulfilling prophecy of inadequacies.
I stayed because I needed to feel inadequate,
because imagine what would happen if I left.
Just imagine…

The End—

Imagine if I loved myself enough to know what
brings me joy.
Imagine if I allowed myself to feel that joy
without the fear of being open.
I am open and raw at this point in my journey,
and I welcome stability—a version of myself
that I haven't seen in years, a cycle I have
decided to never return to.
Peace is something I deserve, so I continue to
surround myself with friends and activities that
make my heart happy and fill my soul.
This was not about her but rather an exploration
of who I was, or rather who I wasn't, with her.
This does not come from a place of bitterness
but rather from acceptance—an end that I must
still heal from because the impact was
long-term.
It wasn't the end that crushed me—it was who I
was in the middle that crushed me.
So I release my soul into these words and
validate my feelings.
This is my story, and it will now live forever as a
testament to my process.

Open mind and open heart…